The Country Pastor

Paraphrases Publishing

The Country Pastor
The Story of Charles Grasty

As told to
Mary Francess Froese

It has been a joy to watch God mature Charles and Debi in their call. I watched him work his way through a major career change and then go on to seminary, where it was hard to balance a growing family and deal with the academic challenges he faced. We worked together in other revival meetings at FBC Neches and have kept up the best we could even after God moved me from Texas to California. Just recently, we had a disaster relief team from the church I pastor in Riverside, CA working in Oklahoma after some of the storms came through. They came home reporting that they met this pastor named Charles Grasty who had asked them if they knew me, when he heard they were from California. It is a small world, but God calls some mighty big people to spend their lives trying to reach it. Charles Grasty is one of those and I am glad to have him as my friend and co-laborer in Christ.

Montia Setzler, Pastor
Magnolia Avenue Baptist Church
Riverside, CA

Geese nesting on Scott's Farm Pond

Contents

Introduction	3
Charles	5
Motorcycle Ride to Repentance	11
Debi....Lost?	15
What! Charles Sing?	19
Give your house to your Daddy	23
God doesn't want our watermelons!	27
Dying to live	31
No more fast trains	39
The Pastor on Horseback	41
The Angel	51
Into All the World	59
East Texas Promise Keepers	73
Epilogue	77
Testimonies of Elsie and Lloyd Grasty	81
Tributes	93
A Last Word	120
About Mary Froese	122

The Country Pastor

Introduction

I have known Charles Grasty for almost twenty years. My California son had moved to the east Texas piney woods and Charles was his pastor. I grew to love this man because he loved my son. Early on, in doing a writing project, I gathered Charles' story on tape and, at my request, he taped him and his wife, Debi singing. The original work was set aside; however, in the ensuing years, I have played these tapes many, many times and have grown to love this man because he loves and serves the One I love. I've played these tapes for friends and we have wept together at the wonderful way God reveals Himself to Charles. This past year his secretary, Sharon Bachelor, and I have known this to be the right time for this book. His is not a story of "coming back" or "coming out," but rather the story of a man who has lived "the good life" all of his life. The good life is "Jesus," pure and simple.

God speaks into the life of this man and people are encouraged, challenged and changed.

He was called to be a country pastor. A country pastor in a little town of approximately 500 souls. It matters not to Charles if they are members of his church, he loves them all. He will minister to any at the drop of a hat. Charles is equally comfortable in front of his computer or donning overalls to help out in a crop crisis or to help in an animal birthing. In the power struggle of our contemporary church, ruled by church growth, self-esteem movements and the politics of the Church at large, I believe the Country Pastor will affect you as a cool evening breeze.

Mary Francess Froese

The Country Pastor

The Country Pastor

Charles

Water hit my hand as it rested on the back of the pew. Opening my eyes, I looked up into his face which was wet with tears.

At the request of the pastor, daddy began to pray for our country at this time of crisis. "Lord, they say we are going to be known as a country that kills its Presidents." As a nine-year old boy, I was hearing my daddy pray for the family of John F. Kennedy. I was gripped by the tears that hit our hands. Daddy's hands were much larger than mine, tanned by the sun, toughened by hard work...but he still had a tender heart toward God and he was hurt for our country.

I had heard him pray all my life, but somehow this time was different. I said to myself, "He doesn't even know President Kennedy, why is he so concerned?"

Daddy's prayer continued, "We in America have sinned and turned from You - even me. I have turned from You and went to my own wicked way and I ask you to forgive me."

I thought, if my daddy who can throw a baseball so much further than me; outrun me; who has hands twice the size of mine; who can lift so much more weight; who can stay up all night long and work; who can take an engine apart and put it back together and it works; who can drive a tractor; who can plumb, weld and build - if my daddy says he needs Jesus, than surely I need Jesus too. I was at the raging river of accountability.

A few weeks later, the revival meeting began (that is when we went to church every night for a week, sometimes two). The first couple of nights were really tough, just sitting and listening. Summer revival especially, for there is no place hotter or more humid than Texas in the summertime.

As the mosquitos buzzed around our heads, we kids made a game of squashing them. After we tired of that we would tangle our legs up together and try to kick them apart.

Finally, it was the last evening of the revival and Sonny Barnhost and I had made it all the way through the service without an adult plopping down between us. We felt quite grown up as we stood to sing the invitation hymn. After the first couple of stanzas I could feel Sonny staring at me. Finally he reached over and whispered, "Charles, are you going to go forward?"

Startled by his words, I jumped and retorted, "Well, no!"

"Then why are you shaking?"

I then realized that my shaking was visible.

"And, why are your hands so white?"

Looking down I saw I was clutching the pew in front of

me for dear life. My heart was pounding so loud I thought sure he must have heard and I felt like all my sins were sticking out so that everyone around me could see. Right then and there I knew that those sins would condemn me to hell.

I looked up and instead of the preacher standing at the front of the church, I saw Jesus. His hands were extended toward me. The choir was singing, "I Surrender All," and the next thing I knew I was at the front whispering into the preacher's ear. The record says I was nine years old.

When I saw those cowboy boots at J.C. Penney's for $14.95, I knew I wanted them. I was about eleven years old when I began to mow yards up and down our street in Houston for a dollar. I almost had those boots, with ten yards behind me and $10.00 in my hands. I was counting my money over and over on the table when Daddy said, "You know, ten percent of that is the Lord's."

"Yes sir! I agreed.

I went back to the bedroom where Mother was and asked her for some change. "I need a dime," I told her.

She did not ask why. Daddy was still reading the Houston Chronicle when I joyfully placed my dime on the table. "What's that?" he asked.

"My ten percent," I confidently replied.

"Well son, your ten percent is a dollar not a dime!"

"God wants a WHOLE YARD!" I exclaimed.

I was at more than a lesson in fractions, I was at a crisis of belief. While I was reasoning it all out in my head and heart, Daddy asked me a few questions. "Where did you get that lawn mower?"

"Out in the garage," I answered.

"Whose is it?" He asked.

"Well, it's ours," I exclaimed.

"I don't think so," Daddy responded. "It's my lawn mower and I'm letting you us it. Now, where did you get the gas can?" he continued.

Just as I started to point to the garage, I realized the next question would be... Whose is it? Daddy read my mind and answered, "That's right! That's my gas can and have you paid to fill it up with gas since you've been mowing yards?"

"No sir," I replied sheepishly.

"No you haven't, but I haven't complained about the gas and I'm happy for you to use my lawn mower. Where did you get your arms, legs, and your good sense to mow those yards?"

"From God," I answered. Well, Daddy had my attention now and he knew it.

"If it weren't for me and God you wouldn't have any money to count right now, would you?" He was right. His words were powerfully right. I could see those beautiful black boots that I was working for. It didn't seem like I could ever get enough money to buy them.

In my room on my dresser, I had a box of envelopes my Sunday School Teacher had given me. As I looked at them, I truly was at a personal crisis of belief. That day I placed a dollar - one whole yard that I had sweated over - in that envelope and signed my name to it. I do not remember what day of the week it was, but it was not Sunday.

One day not too long after that, the IRS man came to our house. In fact, he came two years in a row. He did not believe that Daddy had given the amount to the church that he had reported on his income tax return and wanted to see the check stubs. Daddy went into the bedroom and brought out the "shoe box" and handed him the stubs.

As I recall, that was the first time that I'd ever seen a calculator. He added them up and the total was correct each year. Daddy told him to come back anytime, that he had nothing to hide. Daddy taught me to tithe.

I have been around God's people all of my life. Daddy was a Deacon at Rittonhouse Baptist Church in Houston, Texas. While mother and dad went visiting on Tuesday nights, my brother Clayton and I had Royal Ambassadors and my sister, Wanda, had Girls Auxiliary. On Wednesday nights we

The Country Pastor

all went to prayer meeting. Saturday's daddy mowed the church yard with Clayton helping until he went away to college. It then became my time to help daddy mow - until I was out of high school. However, the most important day of our week was Sunday. Mornings were Sunday School and Church and evenings, Training Union and Evening Service.

My high school years were spent trying to excel in sports. I wanted to be a professional. It really didn't matter what in, so when I threw away my pitching arm in baseball I turned to basketball. When I was too short to excel in basketball I turned to tennis. Although somewhat successful on the court, I still wasn't good enough for a scholarship.

Right before graduation, the class took an aptitude test. I was so intrigued when I got the results, I raced all the way home to share it with the folks. Supper was on the table as I bounded into the kitchen. After prayer I announced, "This test says I'm to be a physical therapist, a minister or a forest conservationist. What do you think about that?" The thought of Charles Grasty, Pastor drew the biggest laugh. The other two certainly didn't appeal... so, like my dad, I became an Engineer for the Missouri Pacific Railroad.

The Country Pastor

Motorcycle Ride To Repentance

It was after midnight as my motorcycle hummed steadily toward my freeway exit. The summer heat had dissipated somewhat and the nighttime sky shone with a clear blanket of stars. Usually this was my favorite time to ride my motorcycle but tonight and for the past few weeks I had become so restless that even this didn't soothe me. In an impulsive moment, I passed up my exit and continued straight ahead. Accelerating my speed, the wind blew through my short brown hair clearing the cobwebs which had been forming in my mind. For the first time in many months my heart reached up to God and I found myself in conversation with Him - a deeply troubled one.

"God, I'm not happy. What's wrong?"

"You are, Charles!" The reply came so rapidly, it was like God had just been waiting for me to ask the question.

In 1974, Debi and I married and we quickly became parents to two beautiful girls, Celeste and Cari. I had a pickup truck, a car and a motorcycle and we were buying a home - life was good. I was busy being a daddy and a husband. I attended church every Sunday I didn't work...but I guess I began to realize I had run off and left God.

Now, speeding along the roadway, He showed me a picture of when I began to move away from Him.

It was late one afternoon and mother was calling me, "Charles, come on - it's time for daily Bible Reading." Clayton was away at college, Wanda was gone from the house so it was just the three of us..

Stepping into my folk's comfortable big bedroom where we usually piled up on their bed to read from the Scriptures, I gulped and pled my case, "Mother, Daddy, I'm thirteen years old now - old enough to read my Bible for myself." Daddy just looked at me. Mother nodded her head, basically giving me her blessing, so I went into my bedroom and picked up my Bible. I felt very in control as I sat down at my desk and began to read. Afterward, as daddy always did, I prayed. Closing my Bible I thought to myself, "Yea, that was great." The next night I did the same thing. The third night, through the cracked door, I just listened to daddy read and pray. The fourth night I did nothing.

Now, riding along on my motorcycle, the pictures continued to crowd my mind as the Lord brought things to my remembrance. He showed me how I began to hold things against my daddy... the times he didn't come to my ball games - yet he always bought my cleats, my running shoes and made sure mother carried me to all the practices and games. He loved to work and provide for the family. He loved me but he didn't love what I loved.

Now, I could see clearly that as I began to grow away from my daddy at 13, I also began to grow away from my Heavenly Father. I don't know how I kept the motorcycle in the road that night. Blinded by my tears, I confessed sin after sin.

God showed me I had not been a good husband to my wife. Oh, I loved Debi but not in a Christ-like way. Just like I saw that I didn't love my dad in the proper way. That night I asked Him to give me that Godly love for my family. Right then, He filled me with a new love for my daughters and a new love and understanding of my dad.

Hours later, a changed man turned his motorcycle into the driveway...a man who once again had power in his life.

The significance really hit home a few nights later. I was reading the paper and Debi stuck her head in the living room and all she said was, "Supper's ready."

Glancing up at her, I gasped. Every ounce of my being was pulsating with love for her. "Lord, she is beautiful!"

Hiding behind my paper, I began to weep, "You DID it!"

The love that God birthed in me at that moment has lasted through the years.

The Country Pastor

Mr & Mrs. Charles Grasty
1972

Debi ...Lost!

My joy at my wife grew. Since I had begun to love her in a Godly way it seemed like all the Scripture says I ought to be toward my wife... I wanted to be. I felt so free to love and enjoy her.

With this new love came a discernment about her that I had never experienced before. I began to notice things about her spiritual life that I had never seen before. I noticed she seemed to lack peace and had no overcoming power.

"Honey, tell me about when you were converted." I asked one day.

"Why!" she retorted.

"This is a very important issue that we should feel free to discuss with each other, honey...now please don't be offended."

"Well, they told me that I was the only one in the Sunday School class who hadn't been baptized, so I just went forward during a service, that's all there is to tell."

"Debi, if that's the case, you just went forward for baptism and not for Jesus. That might account for your lack of prayerfulness. In all of our time of marriage I have never heard you pray first." From the first night of our marriage we prayed together before going to sleep. Debbie would snuggle up close to me, lay her head on my arm and we prayed aloud together. She would never pray unless I asked her to. Now, in my new found discernment, I saw that she loved me but she didn't love God. Her desire had been to please me.

We spent several emotional evenings talking about this issue. "I don't care what you say, I'm saved!" she stormed at me her face wet with hot, angry tears. My tears matched hers as I pled, "Honey, I love you and I just want you to belong to God. We are no longer two people but one, and I am standing before God with fear and trembling for you. I want you to work out your salvation before Him."

She wouldn't budge from her position, so finally I had to let it go, hoping against hope that I was wrong.

A few weeks later, lying on my arm one night before prayer she began to weep. "Charles, you were right, I'm not saved."

My heart skipped a beat, "What makes you say that now."

"I've been thinking and thinking about what you said earlier, and I don't have peace...I've never had any peace. I've always gone through the motions. I've tried to believe I was a Christian and would push any thoughts contrary to the back of my mind. Now, I know better."

Debi came from an alcoholic home where both parents

were heavy drinkers. Especially when she was younger, she craved attention. As I began to put things together in my mind, I saw that, as a young girl, she went forward at a church service more for attention and acceptance than anything else.

Now, lying in bed, I held her tightly until her sobbing stopped and whispered to her, "Debi, Jesus will give you all the attention you ever need," and quietly we prayed that He would fill her with Himself.

In our denomination it is very important to make these decisions public before the congregation, so the next Sunday, it took real courage for my sweet wife to move out of her seat during the invitation, before all of the people she had grown up with, and walk down the aisle to share her news with the pastor. That night as we lay in bed she prayed the most powerful prayer I had ever heard then she began to cry. "What's wrong now, honey?"

"Charles, tonight for the first time in my life I've really talked with God."

The Country Pastor

The Country Pastor

What! Charles Sing?

My head was bent in prayer but I was seeing things. In vibrant color, I saw myself standing on the middle step at Rittonhouse Baptist Church in a navy blue suit, singing my heart out.

Later, on the way home from church I said to Debi, "Honey, I think I had a vision in church today."

"Oh, Charles!"

"I'm not kidding! It was so vivid and I can't get it out of my mind!"

Timidly, I shared with her the picture I had seen and, sure enough, she laughed.

Ever since my motorcycle ride, I had been thinking about some special way I could serve the Lord, since I was not able to teach Sunday School due to my work schedule. Debi has a beautiful voice which she has always used to sing in church so I had said, "Lord, if I could just sing good enough to back up my wife then the world would know that here is a couple who are committed to God and each other." So I KNEW I had my answer. The only problem, everyone knew I didn't have a singing voice.

This had been pointed out to me very clearly when I was a teen. I had just joined the adult choir at fourteen. At practice one of the guys said, "Charles, will you go down to the end of the row, because when you sing, you get me off so far I can't get back on key and then we both sound terrible!" Not being one to wear my feelings on my sleeve, I just laughed and moved to the end.

So, here I was ten years later, God as much as said He was going to do the impossible - give me a voice.

When I approached our choir director to help me sing he said, "Charles, there is no way I would touch your voice..." and he made a big joke out of it.

A few months later the Lord led us to move our membership from one church to another. That church had a music director who not only could sing but also knew the art of singing. He was so good that during the week he performed with the New York City Opera. John Enlow hopped a plane back to New York every Sunday after the evening service. I said to myself after being introduced to him, "Oh, Boy, God! He can teach me to sing." After a few weeks I finally found the nerve to approach him.

"Charles, I commute back and forth to New York City every week. I would love to help you, but I just don't have the time." I was deflated.

By this time almost a year had passed and I was getting desperate. Our pastor lived down the street from us so one day I persuaded Debi to go with me to see his wife, Hazel Meyer, who was also a gifted musician. Maybe she would consent to help me. This dear woman gave me some music and began playing softly on her piano. I took a deep breath and plunged right in. After listening to me sing a few stanzas she stopped and sat quietly for a moment. Looking up at me she said, "Charles, you were low on the first verse and high on the second verse. I don't think you can even hear what I am playing - are you sure it is God who wants you to sing?"

I looked her in the eye and said determinedly, "Yes Mam, I am." Shaking her head she exclaimed, "Well, then I'll have to pray."

As we walked home, Debi blew up, "Charles, I've told you over and over you can't sing...now give it up!"

As soon as we walked into our house, I made for my prayer closet, closed the door behind me and dropped to my knees. I was so frustrated I began to weep. Suddenly I KNEW what was wrong! "Lord, I'm sorry I have failed You! Forgive me. Never again will I go to 'man,' to ask him to do what you have already told me You would do." After a time of cleansing and repenting, the Lord wiped my tears and refreshed me. I had learned a much needed lesson.

About thirty days later I was showering and as always, singing at the top of my lungs. I began to listen to myself. I sounded different! I sounded good! I sounded great! Excitedly, I jumped out of the shower and dried off. Rushing into the kitchen where Debi was cooking breakfast I shouted, "Honey, did you hear me? Did you hear me sing?"

She rolled her eyes, "No, thank the Lord!"

"No, really, I can SING!"

So it was that in 1977, God gave me a voice. From that day forward Debi and I sang for any church that invited us.

We continued to sing in the 60 voice choir. John Enloe must have noticed a change in my voice. I was walking to choir practice one Wednesday night and John said, *Come with me.* So I followed him into large Sunday School Class and he sat down at the piano and said, *I've just picked up this new music. I want you to sing it. It goes like this...* I began to sing along with him. Then he said, *You've got it. Now I want you to sing it to the choir.* He rose from the piano bench and walked across the hall where the choir was awaiting practice. When he walked in he handed the new music to Hazel Meyer sitting at the piano and said *Play this so Charles can sing it.* Hazel looked at John like he was crazy but began to play the song written by Bill and Gloria Gaither, **It Is Finished**:

There's a line that is drawn thru the ages, on that line stands an old rugged cross
on that cross a battle is raging, to gain a man's soul or its loss
on one side march the forces of evil, all the demons all the devils of hell
on the other the angels of glory, and they meet on Golgotha's hill
the earth shakes with the force of the conflict, and the sun refuses to shine
for there hangs God's son in the balance, and then thru the darkness He cries

It is finished, the battle is over - It is finished there'll be no more war
It is finished the end of the conflict - It is finished and Jesus is Lord

Yet in my heart the battle was still raging, Not all prisoners of war had come home
These were battlefields of my own making, I didn't know that the war had been won
Oh but then I heard the king of the ages, Had fought all the battles for me
And that victory was mine for the claiming, And now praise his name I am free

As I sang looking at the faces of my friends in the choir they were smiling. But my wife was looking at me with her mouth open in disbelief. I knew she was right. God had given me a voice ... Suddenly I was overcome ... I couldn't sing the last verse as I was engulfed in tears. The battle was truly over.

Give Your House To Your Daddy!!

When God does something, He does it well. We truly began to live the Scripture, "For our Good and for His Glory". Life was exciting. Debi and I were continually busy with our singing ministry in the Southern Baptist Churches around the Houston area.

After much prayer and believing singing to be our permanent ministry, Debi, the girls and I moved to East Texas and bought some land to build our home. This part of Texas is the most beautiful in the entire state, replete with piney woods and rolling hills. We felt truly blessed by God and we planned by this move to simplify our life style so that I didn't have to worry so much about our income. We would then be able to pursue our ministry dreams of singing in rural churches. In 1981, at Montalba, Texas - the same town where my folks had moved to retire - Debi and I began building our log dream house. My job as a railroad engineer afforded me several days off at a time, therefore, I was doing most of the work on the house myself. Our goal being to have the house paid for upon completion.

Early one summer morning I was rattling toward the site in my old black pick-up. Suddenly, I began to sense the presence of God fill the cab of the truck. Soon the power was so great I began to weep. I was still a couple of hundred yards from the site, but I sensed such an urgency I said aloud, "Lord, I'm coming."

The porch of the house had been roughed in and it had quickly become very special to me as my place of prayer. Every day before I began my work I knelt there to talk over things with the Lord.

Now, I was caught up at this incredible spiritual pull. Hurriedly I stumbled out of the pickup. Overcome with God's closeness, I fell in the recently planted bermuda grass. I found I couldn't stand up so I began to crawl toward the porch. My heart pounding, I pleaded, "Lord, what is it? What have I done?" Again I choked, "Lord, what is it? What have I done?"

After what seemed like an eternity, I finally reached the porch. I was exhausted from the exertion of dragging myself under this tremendous weight. "Lord, here I am."

I waited. After a few moments I heard very clearly in my spirit, "Give your house to your daddy and come and follow Me."

Stunned, I sat there in silence. My house was only four logs high...dad had a completely built home. Finally I said, "Lord, my house isn't even built yet. I wouldn't be giving him anything."

I knew I had given the wrong answer for instantly His

presence left me. I tried to pray and reason with Him but heaven was silent......for months.

At 3:00 a.m., in February of, 1982, my dad and I sat in his car and watched as his house disintegrated before our eyes. The fire trucks had all left the scene. Icy winds rocked our car. Even though daddy was the Chief of the volunteer fire department and all the neighboring fire trucks had responded to the call, by the time they got to us, the fifty mile-an-hour winds had caused the equipment to freeze up. There had been no water with which to fight.. So there we sat.

He sighed, "Well, I've lost everything except for Mama and we've still got the Lord. We have two tractors and the vehicles, so we have more than when we got married."

I felt something tap me on the shoulder. He and I were alone in the car but the tap was so obvious I looked around. The same inner voice I had heard on the porch so many months before said, "Where is your daddy's house?"

The Country Pastor

Celeste, Cari, Charles and Debi

God Doesn't Want Your Watermelons!

The call was intense.

Every revival meeting where Debi and I sang, the preacher would speak on a call to missions, a call to service. It was all around me.

Larry Hargrave, my prayer partner and our guitar accompanist, knew the struggle I was under. "Charles, why don't you give up, you know the Lord has called you to preach."

"Larry, I just want to be sure. That is a very important step and I don't want to go into the pulpit uncalled. And, I'm just not sure if I could handle it!"

We were having a revival in our home church, Montalba Baptist, and as was our custom Debi and I invited the evangelist and family to our home for dinner. Our wives were in the kitchen preparing the meal and Montia Setzler, the Evangelist, and I sat in the living room. "Montia, how do you know when God has called you to preach?"

He grinned, "Well, let me tell you, Charles, God doesn't hide Himself from you. When you are called, you'll know it!"

"Can you surrender late in life, with no education?"

"You can surrender at any time, with no education. Why sometimes people even leave good, high paying jobs and just begin to preach." I felt a shudder creep up my spine.

After dinner, as the Setzlers were leaving, I said, "Montia, I'm sorry we won't be at the evening service tonight, Debi and I have been invited to sing at a neighboring church."

Later that evening, we stopped by our church before heading to the place we were to minister. Larry came up to me as I was loading the back seat of the Setzler's car with watermelons and cantaloupes.

"What are you doing, Charles?"

"I'm just trying to support the Evangelist any way I can... I'm giving him some of my watermelons," I retorted.

"Charles, let me tell you something. God doesn't want your cantaloupes and watermelons, He wants YOU! If you think you are buying time with God by giving these things, you are making a mistake!" Tears started a steady trickle down my cheeks as we stood, glaring at each other.

During the service, after Debi, Larry and I had finished the music, the preacher walked to the pulpit and said, "I've been on my knees all afternoon. I'm not going to preach the sermon I had prepared because the Lord is dealing with one of you here tonight. God is trying to call someone to the ministry, so I'm going to preach on hearing the call of God."

Forty-five interminable minutes later he finally said, "You know who you are, come to the altar." I rushed down the aisle and surrendered.

The Country Pastor

Interestingly, that day Debi and I celebrated our Tenth Wedding Anniversary, July 15, 1982. Ten is the number of completness in Scripture. We were beginning a NEW adventure!

The Country Pastor

Dying to Live

My palms were wet, my knees shook, my mind accused me of losing it as I prepared to again walk the aisle. This time before my home church. Debi held my wet hand. "Here we go...no turning back now!" I whispered to my wife.

We stood at the front of the church, as was our custom, so that the church family could come by and greet us. Some voiced real surprise, others said they had known of this call on my life for along time. All were so supportive.

We had visited mother and daddy earlier in the week to share our news. They were concerned how I, with a wife and two little girls, would manage all that was required to be a Southern Baptist preacher and they didn't hesitate to question us. At the end of our discussion their good faith kicked in and they knew that if God had truly called me into the ministry, He would provide for all our needs.

Before I had heard and surrendered to the call of God, I was already scheduled to preach on Lay Worker's Sunday at Bois 'D Ark Baptist Church. It was very surreal to stand in the pulpit that Sunday, knowing what I now knew. God was preparing me to be used as the Pastor of a church.

The Country Pastor

That night I preached to the men and husbands of that congregation, about their roles in the home and at the time of response at the end of the service, seven women came to the altar to rededicate their lives. The Lord really has a sense of humor. Through the years, Debi and I have had lots of good laughs over that. Preach to the men and the women are touched!

The next Sunday - On August 15th, I preached at my home church, Montalba Baptist Church, and they licensed me into the Gospel Ministry. The following Sunday found me filling the pulpit for the Sheraton Terrace Baptist Church because that week their pastor cut his hand very badly. That same Sunday, in the evening, I preached at Broyles Chapel Baptist Church. A bit later they called me as their Interim Pastor and then further called me as their Pastor.

So once I said, "Okay God, I'm yours!" I've been preaching ever since. I didn't have time to get scared. I was put to work immediately. There is a great need for pastors today. The field is white and the workers are few.

In October, 1982 I was ordained as a Minister of the Gospel.

I continued to work as a railroad Engineer and pastor the Broyles Chapel Church. I was making such good money it really didn't matter if the little church I served paid me or not. Our goal had been to pay off the log house we were building before we moved in to it. But the goal hadn't been met. By this time, we had lived in the house almost a year. We still owed $30,000 on the house and $10,000 on the 55 acres on which it sat.

One day during my weekly prayer time with my prayer partner, a recently retired professor from a Texas University, I just unburdened my heart. He wept as I said,"I really don't know what to do. I know I've got to go to Seminary, yet I don't know what to do about the house. I want to do what the Lord is asking of me." We prayed and my friend assured me he would continue to pray about my dilemma.

One day he called and said he needed to talk with me so I went over to his house. The air was electric as I sat with him in his country home. "Charles, I had a telephone call last week. You know, I have some land in South Texas. I don't even know why I have it. I just pay the taxes on it and it sits there. This telephone call was from a timber man who asked if I owned the land. I said yes, and then he said he would like to buy the timber off it. When I told him it wasn't for sale, he persisted."

"I really want to buy it!"

"Well, what's your price?"

"I'll give you $30,000 for your pine."

"Well, if your going to take the pine off the land, you'll have to take all the timber."

"But I don't want the hardwood!"

"That's the deal. If you want the pine you will have to

take the hardwood!"

"Okay, I'll give you $10,000 for the hardwood."

"Charles, I'd been praying that God would give me the money to help you...The 30,000 will pay the house off and the $10,000 will pay the land off!"

I sank to my knees, the sap gone from my legs. "What are you saying!"

"Charles, I want you to preach the Word of God and never look back. I have no children, no wife, never been married. This is my gift to give and I'm giving it to the Lord, not to you. I have heard you preach and I know that the Lord has His hand on your life. One of these days you'll need a place to retire if the Lord tarries. I hope against hope that He comes soon, but if He tarries you'll need a place. I look upon your wife as my sister and you as my brother. If I have found favor in your sight would you take this offering!"

I couldn't understand what the Lord meant that day on the back porch when he said, "Give your house to your Daddy." God knew all along that He was going to buy the house for me and allow me to give it to my parents. Mother and Daddy lived in that house the remaining years of their lives, They were wonderful caretakers of the house and pecan grove. What a blessing!!! What a blessing!

God had hurled me over my last challenge in beginning my new life

Next stop, seminary. I, again, sought help from Montia

The Country Pastor

Setzler, the one I credit with getting the ball rolling spiritually. He met me at Southwestern Seminary in Fort Worth to plead my case with the officials. Since I hadn't graduated from college there was difficulty getting all my credentials gathered and processed. After my official audience with the seminary admissions we were told that we would be enrolled but not until 1983. I continued my work as railroad engineer, we pastored the church at Broyles Chapel and waited. Dad and Mother were living with us by this time in our completed and paid for log house. In January,1983 Debi and I moved out of our log house and it became my folks home.(Never again have we resided in that log house) We moved to Houston to Seminary housing. I took a leave of absence from the railroad and we began our journey of faith. Oh, boy! Did we begin a journey of faith! I had always made such good money we never had to worry about food or putting gas in our vehicles. We always had money for clothes and fun....

One week we were stone broke. It was coming on the week-end when I was to come back to Palestine to preach - 140 miles. Every Friday afternoon for 2½ years we drove to Palestine to preach - 140 miles each way. On Saturdays I visited, worked around the church, on Sunday we held both morning and evening worship services and then drove back to Houston. We would get home about 1:30a.m. plop the kids in bed and die. The next morning we got the cranky kids up and off to school and I and my cranky wife would attend classes.

Projecting to the week-end we didn't have money for gas to get to Palestine. Debi and I got into a pretty big argument and really is was just tension over not having any money. "Debi, put the kids to bed'" I snapped.

When she came back into the living room I put my hand on her shoulder and shoved her down to her knees. I tell you, if looks could have killed - I wouldn't be here today!

"Don't look at me that way, " I snapped. I'm telling you, you aren't ready to pray - I'm not ready to pray but we're going to pray! I'm coming down there with you."

"Lord, "Here I've worked for the railroad all these years and never gave a thought to putting gas in my car. Now here we are at this seminary. I feel like a duck out of water...Trying to study and make good grades...On the week-ends I'm preaching, mowing the church grass, teaching Sunday School and Training Union, visiting the sick, leading the singing. What else can I do to tell you I love you and want to serve you??? I'm going to have to call that deacon and tell him I don't have money to come there and preach this week-end. You've got me up here with these college students who are all so sharp...Lord, I've been out of school for 13 years and only have one semester of college to fall back on! If you want me to call that deacon I will, I'll put my pride aside. I'm a fool for you, I love you."

The Country Pastor

Before I finished complaining, He began to really hold me in His arms. It was 9:00 p.m. when Debi and I got on our knees mad at each other and mad at God. When we got up off our knees, it was ten o'clock. We went to bed with peace in our hearts. In the prayer, I had also said to God, "Father, you have the cattle on a thousand hills and your servant needs a calf."

Two days later we received a check in the mail. Probably while we were praying those two days earlier, the Lord had spoken to this couple's heart."

The note said, *"Charles and Debi, this is our 25th wedding anniversary. We were going out to dinner and the Lord impressed upon our hearts that we were to give you $25.00. We wanted to send more but the Lord was emphatic that it was to be $25.00 so here it is with our love."*

We received the check at noon on Friday. It took $24.95 to fill up the van. I put the other quarter in my pocket and we fairly flew to Palestine, rejoicing all the way. He had truly given His servant a calf!

The Country Pastor

The family graduates from Southwestern Seminary

No More Fast Trains

I had been on leave from the railroad for the entire time I was in seminary. Now my prayer was, "Lord, I've graduated from seminary. There is so much I need to learn about being a pastor....I really don't have time to work the railroad and do justice to my call. What do I do now?"

While I had been in seminary the railroad had bought out some people's seniority. One of the guys said, "Charles, maybe they will buy yours out."

I went to the union rep and asked him if there was such a possibility. He said, "No way! They have done that for the last time. That won't be happening again."

The next day, at 12:01, the railroad posted that they were again offering to buy the seniority of the senior RR men. They paid me $30,000 to quit working for the railroad.

The Lord made it possible for me to burn that bridge regardless of what a thirty-year union rep said.

I'm teased often about the railroad. The tracks run about 250 yards in front of the church and in the middle of a service when the whistle blows, some of my congregation say they get a little antsy that I might just up to leave the service and hop on that train. Many days the engine idling really beckons. Railroading gets in your blood!.

The Country Pastor

First Baptist Church - Neches, Texas

Brother Charles - Pastor

The Country Pastor

The Pastor on Horseback

Soon after graduating from Seminary in 1987, I was called to pastor First Baptist Church, Neches, Texas. Formerly called Hilltop Baptist Church. Our community has about 600 people in it. Our sanctuary will hold 200 really full. We run about 90 in Sunday School.

I know that I am a 'country preacher.' I consider every person in this community my responsibility. I love them and know them well. I've probably been in every home at least once.

When I surrendered to preach, my only thought was about souls being saved for the kingdom, of preaching evangelistic sermons and singing great hymns of the faith. I never thought about preaching funerals, but funerals have been a real blessing to me. If there is anything that will keep the evangelistic fire burning in my spirit and searching for souls, it is preaching funerals. I am ever conscious that time is short.

Just a few days ago, a forty-year old man threw a chain over an electric wire and accidently electrocuted himself. I had talked with that man time after time about giving his heart to Jesus and he wasn't interested. He is dead now, but my soul is comforted because I had plainly given him the Word of God. Funerals keep you on fire for God!

The Country Pastor

When I was called to FBC Neches, they told me that they wanted to build a new parsonage. That was the least of my worries as I had other things on my mind. I was driving the car that I bought while still a railroad engineer and it happened to be a Mercedes Benz. When I began visiting my congregation and the Neches community I soon found that this was going to cause some difficulties. Often folk would ask, "What....is that your car? Boy, they must be paying you real good up there at that church!"

After I had been here almost a year, I asked a fast friend of mine, Scott Froese, if I could rent his pasture to bring my horse over. He said, "Sonny Boy! I'm having to pay someone to mow it - bring her on over." So, I did....for one reason. I was going to ride her to do much of my visitation. Soon the folks around town had given me the moniker, "the circuit ridin' preacher." If I would drive anywhere, invariably I would be asked, "Where's your horse?" That horse certainly helped me identify with the people of my community.

While riding, I would pray for the families whose houses I passed. There was a spot on the hill that overlooked Neches that I found myself going to quite often, on Bell. I would stop there and pray for the community.

The Country Pastor

Brother Charles and Jan Bryndal, Exchange Student from Poland who lived with the Grasty family

At night, it reminded me of Jesus on the hillside overlooking Jerusalem and how He wept for them. It became my special place of prayer. Even if I was going the other way on Bell, I would ride up to the overlook and pray, first. Often I would find myself sitting in the car on the side of the road at that clearing, looking through the trees in prayer.

Nearly ten years passed. A parsonage site committee had been selected, but for the past two years they had not been able to find a spot to buy and build. A five-acre plot had been for sale for about ten years. The owner had moved off to Ohio.

The parsonage committee decided to see if he would sell part of it. When they called, he wouldn't sell part of it and was asking $18,500. The committee chairman offered him $10,000. To their surprise he took it. It turned out that he was very ill with cancer and just didn't want to be bothered with it.

In a few years, the new parsonage was built and I found myself sitting at the breakfast table blessing our food, looking out over our community from the very spot where Bell had carried me - my own special place of prayer. That particular morning I believe God spoke clearly to me. "You came here to meet Me so often, I thought I would just let you dwell here permanently. My place of prayer had become the parsonage.

The Country Pastor

After awhile I began to breed Bell hopping to get a colt my girls could ride and really enjoy. Sure enough, after the third foal hit the ground,.. there he was! Four white stockings all the way up to his knees...each even! He had a white diamond in the middle of his forehead. A white spot was on his rump, right where his tail came out...which threw a white tail. I took the Children's Church kids down to see him and let them name him. They chose the name "Thunder."

Rand Ivans was a 72 year old man who had moved back home to Neches, where he was born, after working and living in Houston. I soon realized that he wanted nothing to do with me. In a small community everyone knows everyone else...or at least something about him. So I knew his story and was anxious to make a connection with him, but he always evaded me or walked away when I walked into our community store.

I was really concerned about Rand's soul, and had prayed for him for some time. One morning at breakfast I said to Debi, "I'm going to try to walk the colt down Rand's road and see if I can strike up a conversation with him." I jogged the colt, using plow lines to drive him along. By the time we were in front of Rand's house I was exhausted. He was standing in his front yard drinking a cup of coffee. He was attracted to the colt and seeing that I was exhausted, he invited me to set a spell and sure enough, we were able to talk. Sometimes I have to force myself to go slow with the claims of Christ. Better to lay a good foundation than spill it all out and turn a man off to Christ. So we talked and laughed over the colt. I knew when I left Rand that the Holy Spirit had cracked the door of his heart open.

One morning about a week later, the colt somehow opened the gate and got out. When I noticed he was gone, I jumped in my truck to go looking for him. I looked all around the town and then headed up the road to Rand's house. Sure enough, there was Thunder standing in Rand's driveway. When I drove up the truck spooked him and off he ran. Rand hollered, "There he goes, preacher, you'd better go get him before he gets away!"

"Watch this," I said.

I put my fingers in my mouth and let out a shrill whistle, The colt stopped, turned around, and seeing it was me, he nickered and, with head held high, ran wide open the 150-200 yards, back to me..

"Well, if that doesn't beat all! If I hadn't seen it I wouldn't have believed it!" exclaimed Rand. "I was just going into the house to call to tell you Thunder was here, when you drove up! How did you know he was here?"

I put the lead rope on Thunder and suddenly I began to cry. When I regained my composure, I said, "Rand, in my own life I wish I had been as obedient to run to the Lord Jesus each time He had called me, but I haven't."

It was a tender moment and as we both stood there petting Thunder, I said, "Rand, have you ever sensed the Lord calling for you?"

"I sure have, and I've been wanting to talk to you about that."

Rand came to know Jesus as his Savior that day and I baptized him January 16, 1994, at age 72. I asked him if I could preach a little as he was being baptized. To which he replied, "I've waited a long time for this, Brother Charles, you can stand me in that baptistry until my toes shrivel up!"

About a year later he stood in church and gave testimony of how he believed an angel let that colt out of our backyard and led it the mile, up to his house, just so he could get saved.

When Thunder was three, I had to put him to sleep because of Warbler's Disease. A nerve was pinched in his neck and he would fall down. Especially when he wanted to break wide open and run to me when called. He was a wonderful riding horse with such a pleasant personality for people. He would have been loved and ridden by our family for many years to come. It was such a sad thing I had to do, but Rand came with me to have him put down. "Rand, it seems to me like God used this horse for one purpose, to bring you into the Kingdom. His life certainly wasn't wasted!" He nodded, for he was having difficulty speaking. Another very tender moment.

My mother told me that something left me when that horse died. Mother's have insight into their children that is amazing. She was right.

After that special time with Thunder, I lost interest in training colts...even though Bell birthed several others. I knew my kids would be grown and gone before I could get one trained for the saddle, so it hardly seemed worth it.

My daddy died April 13, 2004, about eight years later, and Bell dropped another foal on April 30th. With everything that had been going on, I hadn't noticed that she was close to having a colt. But as God had so wonderfully arranged, mother had spent the night with us. We were living in the new parsonage, on five acres. At breakfast that morning I saw it laying on the ground beside Bell. Mother jumped up from the table and walked out to the pasture as soon as she saw what had happened. I was right behind her. We saw that this colt was identical to Thunder...but this time with a full blaze face. Mother said solemnly, "God loves you, Charles Ray!"

I looked up to her from where I was kneeling, petting the colt, "What do you mean, mother?"

"You just lost your daddy and the Lord has blessed you with a colt the spittin' image of Thunder. I think He's tryin' to tell you something!"

I must admit, I began to weep at the love of God. I felt that in the light of the things that were going on in my life at that moment, truly God was reaching out to me in every way He could to encourage me and assure me that He notices all things. Right then and there we named him T.J. (Thunder Junior). "Charles Ray, isn't that something. God's gonna give you another chance to have what you've lost."

I reminded her that the Bible says, **He will restore the years the locust has eaten.** Almighty God had given me a colt just like Thunder for my grandchildren to ride. Is there anything God will not do to prove His love for those who love Him and are called according to His purposes?

Charles and Debi continue singing
for the Glory of God

The Angel

Nighttime in the country is very dark...and pure. Those of us blessed with living in the country can identify a peace that comes when the only light available is the moon. Sometimes that light can cast its rays with such a warm glow over pasture that one can count the livestock. Stock ponds glitter as the wind rustles the water and has the effects of a nightlight throughout the home. Yet, when there is a new moon, with the tiniest sliver of light, the night takes on a blackness that is palpable. With no streetlights to ward off the blackness, one can sink down into the friendly blackness to sleep a deep and blessed sleep. This was one of those nights. A night when I could have lifted my hand in front of my face and not seen it.

For several years I had been having real difficulty sleeping. This caused great stress on my busy days of ministry. I had been tested for Sleep Apnea and told that I didn't have it. By the time I had gotten to the Sleep Clinic I had already exhausted all avenues one might take to get a good night's sleep... so when I walked out of that Sleep Clinic I was more than frustrated. It seemed that Heaven was silent to this dilemma in which I found myself.

At one point all the medication to help me fight the fatigue had so messed me up, I fell to sleep driving 70 miles an hour. God, in His mercy, protected me as I hydroplaned into a shallow ditch to the right, rather than going into oncoming traffic.

Four years later, our new grandson weighed in at a pound and a half and was finishing cooking in incubators at Baylor Medical Center in Dallas. This meant long drives in heavy traffic to bond with this tiny life. It was while there, I decided to take another stab at the Sleep Clinic.

While speaking with the doctor after being retested he said, "Pastor Grasty, I really hope this doesn't take me to court."

"Whatever to you mean?" I replied.

"It is obvious from the report of the previous test that you have sleep apnea."

"What!"

He was embarrassed and obviously very frustrated as he continued, " Pastor Grasty, I cannot explain how such a mistake was made, because I certainly didn't get these results when you were originally tested four years ago. All I can do is apologize and get you fitted immediately with a C-pap machine."

I went home with eager anticipation that my long-standing problem had been fixed. That night I set up my new machine on my night stand, put the mask on my face and breathed deeply..... breathed deeply.....breathed deeply... I watched the clock tick off the endless hours.

After nine months of this, I took the machine back to Dallas where it was examined. Subsequently, I was told that the machine I had been given was defective every night that I had it strapped to my head.

Another stint with a new machine brought no restful sleep so a year and a half later I was diagnosed with idiopathic hyper-somnia. It has been accepted as my thorn in the flesh as the Lord has not chosen to remove it. It has caused me much misery over the last ten years, with fatigue and memory loss, but has also kept me on my knees.

This night, February 15, 2004, I had immediately fallen into a deep, restful sleep. When I awoke at 2:33, I was jarred back to consciousness. I had been sleeping on my back so my eyes immediately focused on the clock. I was keenly aware of a brightness flooding the room. Every part of my body was rigidly awake. Only my eyes moved, peering to the right of the bed. Somehow I was not surprised to see an entity beside my bed. He didn't seem to be standing on the floor, rather standing above the floor. A foot, hidden by a robe, was propped up on something like a rock. This being's robe was brilliant white. Dazzling! His arms were folded across his chest. My eyes feasted on him for the longest time. He never moved. His presence brought such a peacefulness to my heart even though I felt petrified- turned to stone. As

I lay there looking at him, I didn't know if it was Jesus or an angel. His hands and feet were hidden from view by his robes. I could see where his sash went around his waist because it wasn't as brilliant white there. Or rather, there was an indentation where the golden sash should have been. I could see no face so I didn't know whether I was seeing an angel or the Lord, Himself. Moving just my eyes, I looked at Debi. She was sleeping peacefully with her back toward me.

After some moments I felt maybe I was being disrespectful, just lying there. Maybe I needed to kneel in His presence. However, as I slowly began to raise up in bed, the being dropped his foot off the rock, stood to his full height and was gone. I swung my feet off the bed to the floor and my eyes looked right into the 4 by 8 ft. mirror over our bathroom sink. The image was so etched in my eyes that I still saw the image in the mirror - just like it had been standing erect before me. I looked intently until it slowly faded away and the room was dark again.

I began to talk to the Lord and thank Him for this incredible visit. Though not a word had been spoken to me, the prevailing peace I had in my heart was so powerful that I knew I had been visited by My God. I lay back down and immediately fell into a peaceful sleep. However, even to this time, that visitation is etched into my spirit and I can still feel the import of it.

The Country Pastor

During my life, I have been tapped with a finger twice at night while sleeping. This was to awaken me to pray. Further, I've been touched on my arm, and tapped on my shoulder. Each time I was certain I was in the presence of an angel or the Lord, himself. Each time I would go immediately to prayer, but this is the first time I saw Him. I feel the Lord sent His angel or came Himself to stand by me, encourage and assure me.

During that same week of my visitation, a young man who graduated from Neches High School the same year as my daughter, Cari - some 11 years earlier, called me. I had not heard from him in many years.

While a youth, he had attended our church. He was a deeply troubled child. He did not know who his father was and had never seen him. It took some time for me to find his father and when I did, he denied having the boy. I worked closely with him during those high school years, and even as a child, during Vacation Bible School. We rode horses together and played basketball. I tried to give him a positive male image. So when he called, I was very happy to hear from him after all those years.

He said, "Brother Charles, I'm so glad to finally reach you. I've been trying for days to find you." This was rather puzzling, because I hadn't moved. "Brother Charles, I just had a dream that has really puzzled me.

Can I share it with you?"

"Of course, son, Go right ahead."

"I was in a dark room and couldn't find my way! I was not afraid but I was very confused. Out of the darkness, I heard a voice. Bro. Charles, it was your voice! I said, Bro. Charles, is that you? The voice didn't identify itself. It simply said, 'It's okay, Raymond, come this way!' In the dream, I began to move toward the voice - Your voice. It just kept speaking to him, saying softly,'It's okay, come on.' Finally, I came to a light and could see. At that same moment I woke up. When I awoke, I was just washed in peace."

Raymond went on to tell me that he had just been released, after spending seven months in prison. "I just had to call you - to hear your voice, and to say thank you for all those fatherly talks I had given him through his school years. "You always steered me straight, Bro. Charles. You spoke the Truth from God's Word. I'll never forget it. I guess that's why I needed to hear a familiar voice. Amazing, isn't it? How God let me hear your voice. " We talked for quite a while, and when he hung up, he again knew that he wasn't alone. God sought him out in a very unusual way just to say, "I love you!"

Maybe, I would have been a little skeptical of Raymond's dream, had I not just had my own visitation from God.

The Country Pastor

It is so wonderful. Just ONE WORD from the Master, makes life all better.

Maybe all of the above prepared me for what lay ahead. My dear Dad, Lloyd Grasty, died April 13 of that same year, 2004. I was scheduled to preach his funeral on April 16th. Before the service, many people came and questioned me, "Charles, are you sure you want to preach your daddy's funeral?" Actually, by God's Grace, I was looking forward to it.

The Lord, again, gave me the same peace as he had on that Visitation night. I had such anointing and power as I spoke of my Daddy's influence upon my life; how he pointed me to the Lord Jesus. It is very easy for me to weep during my sermons, as I become overwhelmed with God's goodness. This day was different! My feet never touched the ground as I poured my heart out at Montalba Baptist Church that day. (I give God the Glory due unto His Name!) Only He could have enabled me to do such a thing! When I sang, "The Anchor Holds" at the funeral, my voice never quivered. Not the slightest tear stood in my eye! **My Anchor Held!**

The Country Pastor

Jesus Loves Me

Jesus loves me this I know
For the Bible tells me so
Little ones to Him belong
They are weak but He is strong

I sung this song when I was young
When my heart had just begun
I didn't know very much about sin
But that my life someday would end.

I loved Jesus as a child
And He's made my life worth while
Young or old you can trust Him too
And see what plans God has for you.

Yes Jesus loves me,
Yes, Jesus loves me,
Do ya see Jesus loves you...
The Bible tells me so

Additional words by Charles Grasty

Into All the World

Hunger is the only word one could use to explain the gnawing in my heart. Week-in-and-week out this gnawing stayed with me. Finally in an agonizing time of prayer, I poured out my symptoms to my Friend. And, as always, when we finally get serious in our inquiries, God explained. It was time to go, again!

One can get so engrossed in "his" ministry, that sometimes God has to really set that hunger in motion to get us to think outside the familiar box.

It was 1991 when God really got hold of me to lead out by example into God's world. The first trip to Peru was a wonderful first experience. 1993 it was Australia. What a blessing to bond with 85 other American Christians from seven different states.

We worked with Bega (Bee-ga) Baptist Church. This little church had 35 members. Those members in a period of three months made 1,000 contacts. During the week of revival 45 came to know Jesus as Savior and 20 either moved their letter or joined by baptism! Suddenly their church membership was 100! What a work for God.

The Country Pastor

In 1994 I took my parents on what was supposed to be a pilgrimage to the land of the Bible, This became a joy of all joys as God allowed me to preach and sing throughout "the Land."

Charles doing his thing! Witnessing to a Jew.
Bless God, he heard the Word and wouldn't accept it.
But...the seed was planted.

The Country Pastor

I've been drawn to missions for years, but never before had there been this intensity and urgency.

After God identified the feelings, it was only a matter of inquiry for God to lead me to the group with whom I was to go. The Jimmy Hodges International Ministry was putting together a team of willing witnesses to teach African pastors and their wives. Then the teams were to lead out in crusades.

Arrangements were made and off we went. Teaching pastors in Zambia. What could be greater? What hungry hearts these men of God had. What a joy to encourage them and bring them insights from God's Word. One of the local

pastors had stolen my heart. His name was Moses Zulu. His little church had about fifteen members. Many of the groups met under the trees in the villages. We were there for to encourage, lead out and let the people see that they are important to God and we were co-workers in God's vineyard.

However, as soon as the team arrived in Lusaka Charles doubled over in pain. Dr. Ester Lackey, age 83, had been part of the team. She listened with her stethoscope to say you have a blockage in your colon and it will burst if we don't do surgery. They took me to the Teaching Hospital there. The surgery room was called the theater. When the nurse came over to shave me for surgery she only had a double-edged razor blade. Charles asked, *don't you have a holder for that blade?* She didn't. *Is that a new blade?* Her reply, *This is the only razor I have.* We were right in the center of the aids epidemic. It didn't look good. When she finished Charles called Wayne Lasiter over to his bedside. *Wayne, this is not good. If they don't operate my colon will burst, if they do operate this place is so ill equipped I'll get gangrene and die. Tell Debi that I love her. Tell Cari and Celeste I'm proud of them and that I love them. I don't understand all of this, but I believe God wanted me to come on this trip. I would rather be here in His will and die than be sitting in my living room outside of His will and live. Though He slay me, yet will I put my trust in Him. I want you to pray like Jesus prayed in the Garden ... not my will but Thine.* Wayne prayed quoting Jesus word for word then walked over and sat on the floor. Three men came in and said, *Our x-ray machines don't work. So if you were going to make the incision where would you make it.* Charles said, *Who are you?* His response, *I'm the surgeon and these are students. Well before I tell you where to cut tell me tell me what you are going to do.* When he described his procedure Charles wondered who trained him.

With his finger Charles touched his abdomen where the pain was intense. As soon as he touched his stomach his colon opened up and he began to expel trapped gas. The surgeon said, *Well, the blockage just moved and there is no need for surgery, you can go home in the morning.* God intervened miraculously at JUST the right moment! Charles found out later that his first grandson Braden was born in Palestine, TX at the same time he touched his stomach. (Psalm 37:25) But the battle was not over. As soon as he reached the hotel the team was eating breakfast. Charles ate a soft scrambled egg and his colon went into a spasm and tightened up again.

The Country Pastor

He says it so matter of fact. This doctor has seen God intervene, many times, in this fashion.

I almost faint with relief.

"Pastor Grasty, we both feel that you must be seen at a proper hospital, with proper equipment. God has bought us some time."

The Mission Coordinator, Ben Manis, pulled every string he could and secured a twin-engine plane to transport me to Johannesburg, South Africa. The doctor aboard my flying ambulance is the physician of the Zimbabwe Olympic Team. A proper ambulance is waiting as we land in Johannesburg and speeds me to Milpark Hospital. (All the expenses we have incurred to this point are paid!)

Back In Lusaka, Zambia, I left behind a mission team that is stunned by the outcome of our efforts...but they know how to pray and God built a bridge over their troubled waters.

When I arrive at Milpark Hospital, I am exhausted but before falling to sleep I pray, "Father, I'm sure there must be someone in this hospital that I am supposed to witness to but I am so weak. If You'll just send them in, I will be faithful to witness." That is the last thing I remember until I awaken to see a nurse standing at the foot of my bed. I don't even remember what I said to her, but I'll never forget her waving her hands in the air as she prays the sinner's prayer, finding forgiveness, faith and hope in Christ. I am stunned at her readiness!

That evening, 10:30p.m., Africa time, I talk to my sister in Texas, sharing about the first convert of the trip...and how it occurred...in a hospital! My sister and I have a very special bond that had developed over our childhood and we were extolling the wonders of God....unexpected and strange sometimes, but always wonderful. The nurse, whose phone I was using, had a searching look on her face. When I hung up and handed the phone back to her, I asked, "Do you need to talk to me about the Lord?"

"Yes!" was her ready reply.

"You'll have a break sometime this evening. My room is right down the hall. I'll be waiting."

At 11:45 p.m. Nancy Williams slid a chair up close and I whispered the plan of salvation to her quietly, while an atheist doctor and a born-again Greek Orthodox man slept in the beds next to me. She locked in on every word. I was amazed at her intensity. It was a holy moment as she stepped from the threshold of hell to the threshold of heaven. I leaned forward to hug her neck to welcome her to the Kingdom of God. "How long have you wanted to know the answer to these questions?"

"All of my life!" Was her reply.

At 3:30a.m., I am still so wired by what I have

experienced that I just have to walk the halls. Nurses stop me and ask me to pray with them. By this time, they new me as the "Texan." We talk, there in the quiet hallway, then go behind the nurses station desk and thank God for bringing us together. I see another nurse nearby, weeping. I approach her and ask her name and why she is weeping. "My name is Philie. I'm weeping because God has heard my prayers!!! I've been working this shift for nine months. I've tried to witness to Nancy and Pumla but they would not trust Christ. I prayed in desperation that God would help me. Now He sends a Texan and they are both saved in the same night!"

"Philie, you have the gift of discernment. There are other lost people in this wing. When you meet them, come and wake me, no matter what the time is, and I'll be a faithful witness."

At 5:00 a.m., that same morning, she tiptoes into my room and says, "He's right across, the hall. He is a man from Angola. His name is Chitamba."

I slip into his room. He has a Bible laying across his chest. His arms are weary from reading in bed. "Chitamba, do you understand all that you are reading?" I ask.

"No, I do not!"

I sit down, transfixed by the Awesomeness of God. There are only 8 Southern Baptist Missionaries in the Country of Angola, which is bigger than Texas. I had been in Zambia

The Country Pastor

before I became ill. Both he and I had to fly over two or three countries to get to Johannesburg, South Africa, but God made the arrangements. He put us in the same hospital, then used Philie to introduce us. Right then, right there, Chitamba prayed for forgiveness and to receive Christ. God wrote his name in the Lambs Book of Life...

In the bed next to Chitamba is a very bitter man. He had been ill for nine months. He heard the conversation between Chitamba and myself but said nothing. The next day God moved the atheist doctor out of my room and moved in Mr. Bitter. He was a brilliant lawyer who had been poisoned by his live-in girl friend, who he later found out was a witch. After much discussion, Mr. Bitter came to peace with himself. He was a Christian who had been mesmerized by this woman...and only after he tried to end the relationship did he find out that she was a witch. That morning, God allowed this man to get his life back on track. He rededicated his life to Christ. We were both rejoicing in God's intervention in his life. He gratefully entered into the rejoicing that was overtaking the hospital.

The attending physician felt I should return to the states immediately, for treatment from my own doctor. I just wasn't having any peace about this plan. However, we made plans for the transfer. An ambulance driver came into my room to collect the fee for the ambulance ride I told him that

The Country Pastor

insurance would be paying the full bill and there was nothing to worry about. Instead of leaving immediately, he sort of hung back. Finally he said, "Are you a preacher?"

"Yes, why do you ask?"

"God called me to preach and I was going to seminary, but my father died and I had to quit to take care of my mother. Now, I am doing this secular work."

"Tell me about your Call."

He shared his Call from his Heavenly Father and began to weep as he recounted his failure to finish seminary and follow through with his Call. He felt he had failed God so badly.

I asked him to look me in the eye. Scripture says that the eyes are the window of the heart, and The Spirit confirmed his love for the Lord was real as was his love for his mother. He had been willing to put his life on hold in order to care for her needs. He had never been licensed to the ministry or ordained as he took upon himself the financial responsibility of his mother. As we shared and prayed together, he was released from this sense of failure and the thoughts that God was angry with him. A huge burden was lifted from off his shoulders.

I asked him to kneel and as a minister of the Gospel of Jesus Christ, placing my hands on his head, in prayer I recognized that Almighty God had called him and that had not changed. He confirmed that his commitment to answer that call had not changed either. I spoke to the Lord and said, "Father, if ordination and physical confirmation were needed for Riaan to realize that Your Hand is still upon him, then I ordain him this day in the Name that is above all names...Jesus Christ! Use this young Timothy, Father! May he fan into flames the gifts You have given him. Make Your Mighty Hand on his life known to him this day."

Riaan got up and hugged me and wept out loud. Before he finished weeping, I asked him...is your helper outside born again? He suddenly squeezed me harder and said, "No, I've been praying for him but his heart is hard."

I prayed for the Holy Spirit to break his hardened heart. Just then, he walked back into the room to see what was taking so long I walked over to him and began to share Jesus and he so sweetly came into the Kingdom...it was so tender to hear him pray the sinner's prayer. Riaan hugged him and wept out loud again, saying, "Thank God! Thank God!"

Suddenly peace came to me, It was time to go home An interesting note to this series of events... As I returned home, my very first grandson was laid into my arms. In piecing together the events, we calculated that at the same time the doctor looked at me over the stethoscope and said, "It moved!", my oldest daughter, Celeste, was giving birth to my grandson, August 4, 1995. I praise God that he did not forsake

The Country Pastor

me in my time of need and He did, at that moment, bless my daughter with a son. I have not had any other problem with that type of sickness. I had asked to be an instrument for His glory in Africa...

While I was busy with my hospital assignment, the team of men I went to Africa with, were indeed busy. They reported thousands of Zambians had found Jesus through their crusades. I have a fresh appreciation that our God is Omnipresent!

I would not go back to Africa until 2003. Our charge this time was again to teach pastors and do crusades... This time we took bicycles for the pastors. Our church gave an offering of $1500.00 to purchase bicycles. Our aim for each of the 200 pastors to have one. What fun it was to see all the men of God wobbling about on their new bicycles! Sort of felt like God was enjoying it as well.

After the school we divided up into four teams to 60 crusade locations to preach. The African pastors were great soul-winners, witnessing to everyone they could, while we were setting up the sound system and preparing for the crusade.

The Country Pastor

My sweet Mother, who taught me how to pray for missions, made an afghan with instruction to give it to a Pastor's wife. Moses Zulu was my interpreter in Lusaka Zambia on two different Pastor/Wife Conferences and Crusades and before preaching at his church I presented it to his wife. She was thrilled to have a gift from America. Moses and his children are standing to the right.

The Country Pastor

After the crusades were concluded and all the Pastors had been taught, we found that 11,950 precious souls had come into the kingdom, and 348 Pastors and church leaders had been taught.

I had the privilege of preaching at Moses Zulu's church. I had preached near there the last time I was in Africa, before I became ill. When Moses introduced me, he wept and said they had started with 13 members. Then, after the crusade, their church had grown immediately by 150 members. Now they were running between 350-400 souls.

I had prayed for Moses for the past 8 years and written him, as well. He had the Study Bible I had sent to him. It was so well used that he had already had it rebound!

Oh, that the hearts of America could be so on fire for God as the people of Africa!

The Country Pastor

East Texas Promise Keepers

Someone called the church one day and said there was going to be a great gathering of men at Boulder, Colorado and if I would challenge our men to go, this couple would pay for the gas for the church van. I may have heard about this move to get men of God together, but it didn't really register until I received this telephone call. Always up for a challenge, I approached the guys. Sure enough we had a van load of men to set out for Boulder - on blind faith.

When we arrived, we were astounded to see a stadium full of men... from all over the country. This may be one of the first times some of these men had been to a gathering of non-Southern Baptists. We sat at the very top of the stadium - in the sun - and it became hot! But we were so thrilled to be there...to see what God was doing in the hearts of men. This was a time of challenging men to lay down their secret sins and become the men God intended for us to be. There wasn't a dry eye, anywhere. I've never seen so many men hugging, weeping, hands raised in worship. We drove home forever changed.

The Country Pastor

The following year I had a mission trip scheduled to new South Wales, but the men went back to Promise Keepers. The first year, there had been some 4,500 men gathered as the result of Coach Bill McCartney's dream. We got in on it the second year when there were 22,000 men at Folsom Field.

Now, here it was 1993 and our guys had rubbed shoulders with 54,000 men of ALL denominations and They Were On FIRE!

I've been preaching since 1982 and I'd never before heard men ask if they could pray after church on Wednesday nights. They really didn't ask, they just said, "Brother Charles, we are praying tonight and if we have to carry you to the TEL Classroom, we will."

They wanted me to hear their prayers and listen to all God had shown them. There was so much excitement and energy it was catching. They had experienced a fire in their bones in Boulder. Some of those prayer meetings went until midnight. We even had covered dish suppers with the wives that lasted until 11:00 p.m., and they only broke up then because of concern for the babysitters.

Our men were not all choir members, but they have their own group now and sing amazingly well. The music tells of their joy in Christ and duty to serve.

They go out to other churches, spreading the fire they bought back from Boulder.

The Country Pastor

This is a phenomena that has spread throughout America like nothing I have ever seen.

In 1994, the goal of Promise Keepers was to have one million men praying that the United States would turn back to God. We men from Neches FBC had spoken to 20 churches and we were ready to Go! We filled two buses. Knowing we would need security with such a large crowd, we ordered hunter orange caps for all to wear. With East Texas Promise Keepers emboldened on the front of the caps - we could be seen!

At the first meeting on Friday night, Five thousand men went forward to make a decision of some sort for the Lord. It was phenomenal how the aisles of the horseshoe stadium flowed with men who heard God's call to come forward. Pentecost!

The singing was AWESOME! To hear that many men singing out their love for Jesus absolutely made the hair on the back of the neck stand upright! "Rise Up, O Men of God," "Amazing Grace," "Face to Face," were seared into our spirits. By the time we got to "Crown Him with Many Crowns," I could not sing!

On the last night, Coach McCartney delivered a powerful, moving message then called for the Pastors to come forward. Like a cheerleader he brought over 50,000 men to a constant roar as, I guess, 8,000 Pastors walked forward. I looked back, high on the east side of the stadium and there were my men with the orange hats easily visible. As my tears began to flow, I thanked God for every one of them. I did not know my tear ducts could let flow such a volume. Overcome, I took my hat and slowly waved back and forth. One hat quickly came off to recognize me, then it seemed ten came off at once, then more and more. They weren't just waving. There was so much energy in their signal it looked like a flame of fire on the end of each hand. I could barely stand.

   Someone behind me rested his hand on my shoulder. It was Monte Setzler, the evangelist who had set on my porch swing, July 15, 1982 as I shared that I felt God was calling me to preach. In Colorado, among 50,000 men, standing with 8,000 pastors, at such a tender moment. Look who Almighty God placed right beside me. A man who was with me to start it all!   **Our God is an Awesome God!**

The Country Pastor

Epilogue

On the heels of Promise Keepers, Bro. Charles and the men of Neches First Baptist Church became proactive in the stewardship of their lives. They sought God in prayer, for a way they could reach out beyond the boundaries of their community. The Chainsaw Ministry was born. In August, 2004 these men found themselves in Bartow, Florida to help clean up after a hurricane hit the Florida coast.

Next came Hurricane Katrina and the men made their way to Covington Louisiana, September 2005. They also worked in Kirville, Texas after Hurricane Rita devastated the Texas coast. In January, 2007 they took their chainsaws to McAlester, Oklahoma. They stand ready to go wherever the chainsaw can be a blessing.

Does being a Country Pastor mean you're stuck in the country or that you have time to put your feet up on the porch post and pick your teeth with a weed. I don't think so! Not this Country Pastor! As we have read, he has led out in Mission trips to Peru, Mexico Australia, The Holy Lands, Africa, Honduras.

The Country Pastor

In 2007 he, Debi and several from FBC Neches flew to Alaska to present the Vacation Bible School - Game Day Central!!

Debi and Charles, Alaska 2007

    First Baptist Church of Neches, gave $32,830 to mission causes at home and abroad in 2006.
The Spiritual Charge of this country church says it well,
"Live a life worth sharing - Share a life worth living!

The Country Pastor

◆◆

The Tennessee Colony Prison and five penal institutions are situated within a twenty-five mile area from Neches, Texas. During his prison visits, Charles witnessed the hardship families experienced in coming to visit their incarcerated family members. Many of them had to spend nights in their cars by the side of the road... for prisoners could only have a couple of hours per day to visit and these family members, many times, had traveled long distances to see them so this necessitated staying over night somewhere.

Charles and some of the other area pastors began to pray and seek the Lord as to what they could do to alleviate this added strain on these families. During the time Charles was the moderator for the Saline Southern Baptist Association, he and a pastor friend drove all over praying for some land. They found five acres to purchase and did so. Charles led the association to step out in faith to accomplish this huge project.

This ten-year leap of faith came together in God's good time. Today the Hospitality House is a reality. It is a 50- bed facility that helps thousands of visitors each year who come with children to visit their family members.

The Country Pastor

According to The Barna Group, **one percent** of the American Evangelical Church is made up of the Mega Church/Emerging Church . **Fifteen percent** are Churches of 500 members or more. The remaining **eighty-five percent** consist of Churches with less than 200 members.

This says to me, that the bulk of the work of the ministry is being done by the small church.

This book is meant to testify of the Pastors who continue to seek God on their knees, and congregations who sing "The Old Rugged Cross" with gusto. And where folk are still bowing their knee to a saving knowledge of Jesus Christ.

Our God is looking for a "Few Good Men" who can be shepherds to small flocks..... In looking at the life of Charles Grasty and the ministry of First Baptist Church of Neches, Texas, may you be challenged to accept or renew the Call of God on your own life.

M.F. Froese

Testimony of Elsie Marie Vannoy Grasty

Elsie was born in 1922. Reared near Palestine, Texas. She came from Godly stock.

I'm thankful first of all that God gave me strong, Christian parents who taught me right from wrong. One summer, when I was a teenager, we were having a revival. There was a tabernacle between Mrs. Ivy Richardson's house and the Christian Church. It was a roof set on poles with a sawdust floor, but no walls. Bro. Stephenson was the evangelist.

I was sitting kind of in the back with some other young folk and I remember walking forward and telling Brother Stephenson that I wanted to accept Jesus as my Savior. Nobody coaxed me and I walked forward by myself. I knew that I had sin in my life and I needed to ask the Lord for forgiveness. I was baptized in a creek on Carl Hanks' place, east of Montalba.

After high school, daddy and momma sent me to a beauty college in Dallas. I had never been away from home before, and Dallas was so big and so different from what I had been accustomed to. I lived with a young married couple with three little children. I took care of the kids for my rent. I had to stay out of school one day a week to help her clean house;

in addition to bathing, feeding and watching the kids every day after school. They didn't go to church. They partied every week-end.. Every once in awhile, I got a Sunday off and rode the trolley car to church.

When I first got to Dallas, I knew the street address where I was to stay and where the beauty college was. I rode the trolley car back and forth. The first week I rode the trolley home it was so crowded that I couldn't see the signs. I was too bashful to ask the driver to tell me when we came to my street. I thought we were there so I got off. As the trolley rolled off, I realized it was the wrong street. I knew I was in trouble. I didn't have any money and didn't know anyone.

I walked out in the street and got in the middle of the trolley tracks and started walking because I knew the tracks ran by the house where I was staying. I walked and walked. It started getting dark and I wasn't there yet. I began to run because I was supposed to be helping with the kids, getting their baths and reading them their story. God knows I ran until I gave completely out. I never was so glad to see a street sign in my life! I got there right at dark - give slap out!

After I put the kids to bed and got them to sleep, then I would get my lessons. I would pray myself to sleep asking God to help me make it through another day. The experience really made me trust the Lord. Momma and Daddy weren't there to help me and I got close to the Lord during that time.

The Country Pastor

I had never been away from home. The people that I stayed with partied during the week if they could find a place, as well as on week-ends. They left me there with the kids by myself. I never told mother and daddy that I was scared 'coz I knew they couldn't do anything about it.

I never will forget one day when I saw their old truck coming to check on me. They brought food and we went out to a park to eat and visit.

Three weeks before school was out, we had classes at night and they had us to study on the questions that we would be asked at the state board. Five of us girls rented an apartment together to study for the finals. It was close to school. Every one of those girls would go off and party the night away. They were smoking and drinking and had boyfriends coming over. They tried to get me to go with them, but I flat wouldn't go. I tried to get them not to go, but they wouldn't listen.

Young people! I want to tell you that you will never be sorry about behaving. The sooner you learn that the Lord is watching you all of the time, the better off you will be.

Talk to the Lord Jesus in prayer. Learn to trust Him. Obeying your parents now will only prepare you to obey the Lord for the rest of your life.

Written January 25, 1998 at age 76.

Lloyd and Elsie Grasty

The Country Pastor

Testimony of Lloyd Grasty

My family moved to where the Land of Memory Cemetery is now when I was five years old. Where the graves are now was all field and we worked it. We raised cotton, corn, peas and made syrup. We started school over at Broyles Chapel when we were seven. Mr. Dick Humphrey, John Link and Dillard bought a truck, put a bed on it and made a school bus out of it. Mr. Link's oldest boy drove the bus and he was going to school there too. It was up and down the clay hills and we'd have to all pile off and push. There were about 20-25 of us kids that sat on that flat bed and rode to school.

Daddy bought a Model T, stripped down without a bed or a cab. We had to build a bed to go on it and a cab too. No windshield. We'd go to church on another Model T truck. We'd sit on the gas tank because there was no cab on the truck. My oldest brother learned to drive it and we'd pick up kids on the way. The little ones sat in the middle with the older kids on the edge to keep the little ones from falling off. We'd have 15 to 20 on it before we got to church - all happy for the ride.

The Country Pastor

Lone Pine Baptist Church didn't have a wooden floor. We just had sawdust shavings. We used carbide lights. We used lamps a long time before electricity came out there from town. We used funeral home fans and lumberyard fans for our air conditioning. When I was a teenager, one of the preachers was Marvin Johnson. I was sixteen years old when I was saved, August 7, 1935. There were sixteen of us baptized in Six-mile Branch. Brother Johnson's preaching and my faithful Sunday School teacher, Mrs. Nellie Carpenter, were used by the Holy Spirit to put me under conviction. She lived near the church on the highway, but it was about two miles back down the creek where we had the baptismal service. We'd get baptized and then the boys all stayed and swam awhile.

Papa farmed on down the creek and damned it up. He grew ribbon cane and had a syrup mill. Dillard and Papa carried 500 gallons of syrup out to West Texas and sold it for a dollar a gallon. Ribbon Cane was the highest priced syrup there was back then.

T.W. Wright was the vocational and agriculture teacher. He taught me how to graft pecans on hickory trees. We had a project that we built a wagon from the ground up and painted it green and yellow just like it would have been if we had bought it. We sold it to someone and helped buy something that the school needed. I played basketball and I was never good enough to play on the first team, but I enjoyed

The Country Pastor

it. Jim Thompson was an ace player. He could flat make a bucket. Winfred Green, Billy Kelly, Dawson and W.T.Lightfoot, Aleck Huddleston, Homer Williams and Ned Johnson were some of the players. I went through the tenth grade but they didn't have but eleven grades back then. Lois and Elsie Vannoy got to be good friends. Elsie started coming to our house and suddenly my mind was on something besides school.

We raised hogs, cows, and chickens. We farmed with mules on forty acres on the hill towards town and 160 acres at the cemetery. Our family could pick a bale of cotton a day. The first job I had I went to work for a filling station at night from 7p.m. to 7 a.m. I made one dollar a night for 12 hours work. That was seven dollars a week. After I left the service station, I went to work for East Texas Cotton Oil Company, which was later sold to Swift.

Elsie and I were married at Tom and Lula's rock house in Montalba. Howard Hilton and Pauline Butler stood up for us. We rented a furnished apartment on North Jackson and didn't have a car when we married. Tom Vannoy carried us to town and we paid rent on the apartment and walked to get groceries. Just as we got ready to go to bed, a loud knock came at the door. It was Howard and Pauline. They stayed until 2.am. Aggravating us, talking and laughing. They kidded us later about how they held up our honeymoon.

The Country Pastor

I was making .35 cents an hour at Swift. Later I left there and went to work for the railroad as a machinist helper at .68 cents per hour. Every six months I received a .06 cent per hour raise. Somehow Elsie and I got to Houston without a car and rented an apartment downtown on Leland St. We stayed there for three months and I was hired as an apprentice machinist in Palestine for .35 cents an hour so we could live back home. After I worked about two years I got promoted to a machinist at .96 cents an hour.

Once promoted, I would work on the road or on Saturday's and Sunday's. They couldn't work apprentices on the week-end or pay overtime back then. When I got that job, I bought a '54 Mercury. We were living on Conaway Street and bought two lots side by side. They quit having school up at Bois D'arc and I bought the old school building for $1100 and built our house out of it. When I got through, I had half of the lumber left. Lloyd and Lucille Fitzgerald used it to build their house up where Uncle Jim and Aunt Clara later lived.

I worked as a railroad machinist for several years during the steam engine days. Then I became roundhouse foreman and worked on a swing job. I also worked Saturdays and Sundays over at Mart and a night or two in Palestine relieving Stumpy Jones.

Later I changed over to transportation and hired out as a

The Country Pastor

fireman. That sent us to Houston again. This time we bought a house and began to go to Rittenhouse Baptist Church. Clayton was saved soon after we arrived and Wanda and Charles Ray came to Christ later on.

The preacher encouraged building a family altar, so Elsie and I would call the kids into our bedroom and we would have our devotions and pray together. I was ordained a Deacon there and what a fine church family we had. I mowed the church lawn with my tractor because I felt that God asked me to. That was 13 acres of mowing for 13 years. Clayton helped when he got old enough and so did Charles Ray.

I made extra money with bees. I wound up with 60 supers of bees. This kept Elsie and the kids busy helping me extract honey to sell.

In 1970, when Charles Ray graduated from high school, we moved back to Montalba and plugged right in to the Baptist Church there. We were happy that the Lord let us move back home.

I've always loved to garden and to me, working for the Lord is like gardening in God's Kingdom...all for His glory! I don't see how anyone would not want to return the tithe to Him. To keep it is stealing from the Lord. And who would not want to serve Him and show our appreciation to Him. Jesus gave His life for us on the cross.. There is no better place to serve such a wonderful Savior than in a local church.

He's the One who formed the Church in the first place. It's beginning was His idea. If you quit the Church you'll have to tell Him why one day, when you stand before Him. I'll be the first to say that I'm a sinner saved by His grace. That's what the Church is made up of. I'm not worthy to serve Him, but I can't think of anything better to do with the life He gave me. Everybody knows people need the Lord. It's our job to get the word out.

The Grastys' Pride and Joy minus one
(Back to front)
Caden Mullican, Jordan and Braden Davis
Colton Mullican not pictured

The Country Pastor

Tributes To a Man of God

The Country Pastor

Celeste Oliver

My dad is everything a dad is supposed to be. He is loving, caring, understanding and he has always been there for me. Most of all, in growing up, he prayed with me every night at bedtime. I remember as a child we would have family devotions and mother, Cari, daddy and I would all climb onto their king-sized bed and daddy would ask each one what we were mad about, sad about and glad about. I remember that those devotions would last a couple of hours. It was really amazing how that time we had together at night as a family brought us closer - very close.

My dad was always the one who made sure that we had whatever we needed for school, church and home. Also, he made sure that we went to church together and if my sister or I had questions about a sermon or Sunday School lesson he would explain and make sure we understood.

He believes that a family who prays together, stays together. My dad made sure that we, as a family, knew that we were supremely loved by him, but most of al l- that God loved us. What matters most to me is that I will always be daddy's little girl.

I love you daddy!!!

The Country Pastor

Cari Mullican

I learned from my daddy that you can talk to God anytime, anyplace and while you are doing most anything. Daddy usually drove Celeste and me to school each morning. This was our special time. We would talk and say our morning prayer together. Most of the time Daddy would say the prayer because my sister and I were not fully functioning, yet. I can remember one morning I began thinking, how is daddy driving and praying at the same time? I had always been taught that you pray with your eyes closed. Now I know how ridiculous this must sound, but seriously, I was curious, so I peeked at my dad to see how he was accomplishing this task. I was so amazed! I thought, "Wow, we can pray with our eyes open." Many years passed. I received my driver's permit and I got to pray with my eyes open. It was really cool. In fact, now at 32, I still pray while I'm driving to work in the mornings and yes, with my eyes open.

    Daddy and I would talk about the choices in my life, whether about school, friends or life. My dad would not tell me what decision I should make, but he would say to me, "Cari, when you please God, it doesn't matter who you displease." I learned from daddy that pleasing God was always the most important and right choice to make. When I've had a tough decision in my life and the right decision was not the easiest to make, I would think back to that quote and say it to myself and then I would find the courage to make the right choice. I wish that I could say that I have always made the right choice.

Another life lesson my dad taught me was about God's grace, mercy, unconditional love and learning from your mistakes. He also showed me how to ask forgiveness of my sins, a lesson that is used daily. "Thank you, Lord, for your grace and mercy!"

My dad never let my sister or me say the words, "I can't." He never let us quit anything to which we were committed. I'm so thankful for that character builder, for living the Christian life can be very hard. We all go through storms in our lives; daily, monthly and there have been brief moments I have wanted to quit. But, I continue to persevere just like my dad has continued to persevere in his walk with the Lord and in his ministry.

Thank you Daddy for treasuring the two gifts that God gave you and Mama (Celeste and me). And, thank you for obeying God, by raising us in a Christian home with Godly values.

Your daughter, **Cari**

The Godwins

We have known Charles Ray since he was a teenager at our church. Everyone liked him, due to his outgoing personality and love for people. He showed admirable qualities in his dealings with people and with life circumstances. We were privileged to attend his and Debi's wedding.

Bobbie and I felt it to be an honor to be their Sunday School teachers in the Married Young Couples Department where they were very faithful.

Charles Ray planned a long term career with the railroad but found that God had other plans for him. Charles' surrender to God's call to the Gospel Ministry has been a great blessing for so many whose lives he has touched. He truly has a pastor's heart.

Our lives have been so blessed through the friendship and fellowship we have enjoyed with Charles Ray and Debi. We have watched with joy as he has grown from a teenager into the man of God he is today.

We pray God's richest blessings on Charles Ray as he celebrates his 20th anniversary in the ministry.

Jim and Bobbie Godwin

The Country Pastor

Wayne Lasiter

Everyone needs help on this journey called the Christian Life. I have been blessed to have the help of my friend Charles Grasty. I could share so many stories of prayer times, mission adventures and heartfelt conversations, but I will speak of just one story that impacted my life. I was pastor of Montalbe Baptist Church in the early 90's. I was trying to get an education at Southwestern Seminary, preach three sermons a week, visit everyone I could, and try to be a husband and father. After about a year and a half, I found myself exhausted and frustrated. One day, I was having lunch with Charles' wonderful parents when Charles drove up. After lunch, I told Charles how I was doing and asked him for advice. His reply was quick and to the point: "Boy, you are burning out and there is only one cure for it: You must walk with God."

I quickly realized that I had been neglecting my time with the Lord. I had time for so many other things, yet had neglected the most important relationship of all. No wonder I was worn out! It was amazing what a fresh word from the Lord - through a good friend can do for you. I began to spend more time with the Lord and to desire to walk with Him.

I had new found strength and peace. It has been my experience since that timely word from Charles, that whenever I truly walk with the Lord, I have everything I need for this life; when I don't, I find myself in trouble, frustrated, and exhausted. It has also been my experience that my friend Charles Grasty is a man well acquainted with walking with God, for his path has not always been straight or easy yet he faithfully practices what he preaches. He truly walks with God.

The Country Pastor

Richard Waters

You were there when our Palestine experience began - with friendship, prayer and the love of a fellow pastor. Then there was your loving family - your deacon father with his wisdom and you mother with her kindness, your dear sister with all her sincerity and prayerfulness, your brother-in-law, Lee Bishop, who was a member of the search committee that found and presented me to the First Baptist Church of Palestine. It was always helpful that you knew and understood the people of FBC so well, making your thoughts and prayers so very valuable to me along the way.

For us, you and me, there were great times of fellowship and prayer. I recall just before I left, I was getting down hearted. You and I visited for a long period of time at the cemetery. You seemed to understand and care so very deeply. I was always honored when you would share a bit of your own heartbreak and burden with me. Through some really tough times you maintained your love for Jesus, and your strong commitment.

Aside from our personal friendship, there were those times of sharing ministry, that God used in both our lives greatly. There were the men's breakfasts which helped so very

The Country Pastor

much in the beginning by the Promise Keeper ministry which you lead. Remember when you and your men came to testify and sing at FBC. Our young men were ignited by that ministry. Ken Rawson is where and what he is today, in large measure because of the Promise Keepers of East Texas. I still have that bright orange cap you gave me to identify us in the vast crowds in the stadium. There was your love for missions. I encouraged you to go with JHMI on mission. My, what a mission that was! You almost died - but how God used your witness will be told in Glory, some day. This all makes me so very grateful to call you my dear friend.

There is a song that makes me think of those days of ministry in Palestine, and of you my dear brother, "May those who come behind us find us faithful." These twenty years as "the country pastor" have earned you the great compliment - Charles Grasty - Faithful Man of God. You are a faithful husband, father, grandfather, son, brother, pastor, Christian leader and friend.

Congratulations on completing twenty faithful years of ministry to the Glory of our Wonderful Lord and Savior Jesus Christ. Gratefully and

Onward!

Toward the time when the Day Star shall appear and we shall meet at His Dear Feet.

Richard Waters,
Friend of Charles Grasty

The Country Pastor

Sharon Batchelor

I was a very timid young mother who walked into the church office in 1990 to begin working as the part-time secretary. The first week with Bro. Charles had me ready to quit when he told me that he and the previous secretary always prayed in the office on Monday's. How intimidated I was, having not prayed out loud with very many people, let alone a seasoned pastor. Little did I know just how much this man prays and for how long. Once he finished, I would struggle to even think of anything left to pray for! I can say I have heard every person's name in our church called out regularly in prayer. This is a man of prayer .

His burden always includes the lost; that they too would come to know the saving grace and forgiveness that he experienced as a young child. His passion is to see others come to Christ. I'll never forget coming to the office at thirty years old and talking to Bro. Charles about my doubts and fears of being unsure of my salvation. He had me hold the Bible in my hands and pray, "Lord, this is all that I have to hold on to and I believe You are who You say You are. I believe Your Word is truth. You are not a liar, and You will do as You promise; the Bible says You are able to save me. " There in the office, I trusted Christ to be my Savior.

The Country Pastor

I thank the Lord for this man of God who faithfully shares the Gospel.

My family has truly been touched by his and Debi's love and friendship. We've laughed until we've cried at all the stories of "Mama" and growing up in Houston and Montalba. I always think of Mrs. Grasty coasting down Bowden mountain to save gas and losing power steering and brakes, throwing her groceries in the floorboard and breaking her eggs, and narrowly escaping with her life! Then, there is the dentist office story! My kids loved riding on Bro. Charles' boots at church, giggling down the hallway as he held their hands to hang on. How many hours he spent riding horses with Lindsey and teaching her about the important things of God. They would go over to the pecan orchard in Montalba and ride the golf cart down to "the altar" tree and pray. Someone once commented after hearing Lindsey pray, "Bro. Charles must have taught you to pray."

I asked Lindsay what words come to her mind when she thinks of Bro. Charles, and she immediately said "selfless... He always has time...willing to help. He is so honest and real...a good example in the way to approach God. He thinks of what you like and shares his possessions and time... He is a hard worker. He is funny, a great story teller with his Mama's tales. He is always involving others in what he does. He cares."

Our family is forever grateful to Bro. Charles for the

impact he has had on our lives. We can never measure the investment he has made in our family's spiritual growth.

For the last 17 years, I have had the opportunity to see the 'behind the scenes' Charles Grasty. I haven't seen a perfect man but I have seen a consistent man of integrity and faith who has such a heart for Jesus Christ and His people....lives which have been touched for eternity. I know mine sure has.

"Dear Lord,
Thank you for loving Neches so much that
You sent your anointed and chosen man,
Charles Grasty, to come and invest his life by
faithfully working among us these past 20 years;
showing us, 'The Way, the Truth, and the Life',
that we can have through Jesus Christ, Your Son.
Oh God, bless all your pastors today, that they too
will not grow weary in well doing...but finish the
race - strong that You have laid before them. To
You, Oh Lord, be the Glory - forever and ever."

Bro. Charles, what an honor to call you my Pastor, my friend, my boss, my neighbor, my brother in Christ. I am joined in appreciation with the little boy in Africa who called out to you, **"Mr. Texas, Mr. Texan, Thank you for coming across the water to bring me this "Good News!" Isaiah says, "How beautiful on the mountains are the feet of those who bring good news."**

Much Love, Your Secretary

Manning Garrett

My wife, Waime, and I have high regard for both Charles and Debi. In fact, when our children were all young (we have 4) it occurred to us that should we both die, we needed to designate someone to care for our children. Immediately, we thought of Charles and Debi. We could think of no better Christian couple to raise our children, should we die, than this fine couple. Thankfully, we never had to cross that bridge. Nonetheless, our feelings and impressions of Charles and Debi remain the same.

My path in ministry has been different than most men. In the mid 80s, Waime and I began to sense that perhaps the Lord was leading me into a teaching ministry as well as the preaching ministry. We did not know how I could achieve the necessary education, given the fact of our age and that we had a family to support. In 1986, at Southwest Baptist University in Bolivar, Missouri, Charles joined me in a prayer meeting for the Lord's leadership in this important matter. At midnight, we knelt at the fountain in the middle of that fine campus and prayed for God's direction for my ministry. When we completed our long prayer time, I rose to my feet and knew that God would open the appropriate doors at the right time. That experience with my friend Charles has become for me a bench mark tracing God's plan, especially when times are hard and I do not sense God's presence as profoundly as at other times.

I not only consider Charles a dear friend but I also regard him as a bit of a mentor in terms of what a pastor ought to be. I have learned to pray by listening to Charles pray. I have learned to value quiet times with God because I know that my friend has met God in an intimate way when he has spent time alone, with Him, "wrestling" with spiritual and personal issues.

Charles has preached revivals for me in all of my churches that I have pastored in Louisiana, Georgia and Tennessee. In every church, the people always ask, "Do you think Brother Charles would come back again and preach a revival for us?" In fact, as I am typing these comments, Charles is driving to Jackson Tennessee to preach his second revival in my church, the East Laurel Baptist Church.

Anyone who has ever heard Charles preach knows that he has mastered the art of "spiritual communication." I do not mean entertainment. I mean that when Charles preaches people know that they are listening to a man who knows God and believes deeply in the truths that he is sharing. The tears that run down his cheeks while he preaches flow from a heart that sincerely cares for those to whom he is ministering. His stories and examples are not 'book read' they are 'life led'; they flow

The Country Pastor

from over two decades of ministry where his life was touched the lives of thousands for God and for good.

In closing let me add one more conspicuous point. I have never met a man who seeks God's will as much as Charles and Debi in the matter of 'when to leave a church.' For two decades Charles had been the pastor of the First Baptist Church at Neches, Texas. Numerous pulpit committees have contacted him from larger churches. Only one thing matters to Charles and Debi; Does God want us to leave Neches. Charles knows the heart of God in matters such as these, because he searches for God's will like no pastor I have ever met. His example has inspired me to do a better job of seeking God in prayer. I believe that I am right when I say that Charles and Debi will be where God wants them because they will know God's will before making a major decision.

Without going into the details, let me add one final thing. Charles has provided me with practical, spiritual counsel on several occasions. I am a private person and by nature a philosopher, which means that I am skeptical of a lot of what I see about religion. Charles is the only pastor that I confide in because I know that he is 'the real deal' who seeks first and foremost to please God. He and Debi have made many financial sacrifices to do what God wants. When I have needed a pastor, Charles Grasty is the man I count on for advice, example and prayer.

It is an honor to write these laudatory comments about my friend, Charles Grasty. May God continue to use him and Debi in His ministry for many years to come is my sincere prayer in Jesus Name.

L. Manning Garrett III, Ph.D
Assistant Professor of Philosophy and Religion
Lambuth University
Jackson, Tennessee

Barbara J. Hassell

I respect Bro. Charles. He has made a positive impact on my life with his insight into the Holy Word of God. I always looked forward to the many times we spent in our conversations. We'd pray, laugh, and yes, we also did some weeping right there at the Post Office counter. I confided in him, shared some of my concerns about people, and he with me. He ministers not only to his own flock, but to all people of the community. He is truly a 'people's minister.'

He would find a way to communicate with a person, even used riding his horse to put people at ease with him.

Once Bro. Charles told me about a young girl who had problems with a young boy wanting to date her, when she really didn't want to date him, but she also didn't want to hurt his feelings. Bro. Charles told her to say to him, "I don't date unless you are a possible mate, and you are not a possible mate for me." That ended the problem!

Once, I received a card from him which said, "It is wonderful to have a born again Postmistress."

Three years after I retired he wrote, "I miss the 'pauses' from life we had to worship. I could always see the love of the Lord in your eyes."

I shall never forget the time I was invited to their home to spend the night. He, Debi and I stayed up late talking and enjoying Christian fellowship. That was a 'special' moment in time for me.

A quote I remember:'*Sin will take you further than you want to go, and keep you longer than you want to stay.*' And as he always signs off with, 'Live a life worth sharing -.Share a life worth living!'

I just want to say to Bro. Charles, 'You are a very dear, sweet man who loves God and His family, and I love you like a brother!'"

Barbara J. Hassell
Neches Postmistress, retired

The Country Pastor

Hazel Meyer

Charles, I cannot believe this is your 20th anniversary in the ministry; however, time flies and we fly along with it. Was it that long ago when you used to write letters to me as you rode on the job on the train? I suppose it was and you were just a kid, puzzling over what the Lord wanted to do with your life. You and Debi lived across the street from Leroy and me while we at Hidden Valley Baptist Church.

You and Debi were members there and in the Sunday School class I taught. Debi had such a beautiful singing voice and one day the two of you came across the street to our house. You announced that the two of you were going to sing a duet at church and would I practice with you. You had already picked the song: I played the introduction and you started to sing. Now, there is singing and there is singing!

I thought you missed your note, so suggested that we begin again. However, it was the same result. Finally, after pounding on the note that was to be yours and got the same results, I thought, "This is NOT going to work!" I suggested that we work on it a bit more before you decided to sing. I could tell that Debi didn't know what to do. We did nothing and the next thing I heard about your singing; you had gone to the Holy Land and was asked to sing, "How Great Thou Art."

I couldn't believe it! Not only were you preaching, but

you were SINGING AND on KEY! Later when I heard the two of you sing, I just cried and praised the Lord for what He had done in your life! You prayed to be able to sing and He said yes! Isn't that just like Him. He does the unexpected and it glorifies Him.

I am so thankful for you and for the obedience you have continued to show to Him. My prayer for you is that you will always follow His leadership and have the strength to follow where He leads.

There is such happiness and contentment in following and obeying. "Trust and obey, for there is no other way to be happy in Jesus, but to trust and Obey.

My love to the both of you,

Hazel Meyer

The Country Pastor
Terry Nied

"Thank you for giving to the Lord." The first time I saw Charles Grasty was in September, 1997, at a revival at Montalba Baptist Church. This tall, impressive man started singing, "Thank You," by Ray Boltz at the rear of the church. As he came down the center aisle, placing his hand on some of the elderly of that church, he sang in perfect pitch the beautiful words of that song. I didn't know Charles Grasty, or, have any idea of the future impact of his ministry on my life. All I knew was that the words, "Thank you for giving to the Lord," and his presentation of those words, caused "goose-bumps" to rise on my body and I found tears in my eyes. Those tears reoccur, even now, as I say "Thank you for giving to the Lord," Charles.

Our paths crossed later at a Dogwood Trails Area Christmas party at Frankston. This tall preacher approached me as Lorie and I were leaving, about giving him guitar lessons. At that time I was a church musician at Broyles Chapel Baptist Church. "I'd like to play guitar at church and I'd like you to teach me," Charles said. My heart was touched by his sincerity to serve the Lord. On the following Friday nights, Charles and I would meet, usually at the Neches parsonage, and play and sing. There was a little instruction, a little singing, and a lot of prayer. I discovered that hours would pass when Charles prayed for me. While parts of my anatomy were suffering numbness, the thoroughness of Charles' prayer was a blessing. Charles has the gift of compassion, and we wept together as he prayed for me, and the church he loves so much. Nobody that I know prays like Charles. I would label his prayer style as "direct conversation with the Lord." As it turned out, I needed his prayer much more than I knew.

It was at one of these "guitar lessons/home worship services" that I posed a question to Charles. "Charles, what was it like when you were called into the ministry?"

"Terry, do you think that it happening to you?"

I had been to Alaska on my first mission trip, and God had begun to call me into the Gospel Ministry. The facts were clear - I had tried to run from God and the Call, but there was no place left to run. I was wretched, exhausted, and vexed in my soul. "Yes, Charles, I think that is what is happening, and I cannot afford to be wrong with this! Am I going crazy? "Terry, it will be different for you than me. All I can tell you is that when God closes a door behind you, He will open one in front of you, and there won't be several doors in a row opened before you. When He opens the door, <u>Walk through it,</u> Terry."

That night the prayer time extended past midnight, and I surrendered to the Gospel Ministry in the quietness of my home. I later made that surrender public and was licensed and ordained by Broyles Chapel Baptist Church. I was called to

Calvary Baptist Church five months later, were I currently serve as Pastor.

Since that time, my friend has ministered to me continually, as the Apostle Paul did to Timothy, his son in the ministry. This continues to this day, with no end in sight. We have traveled a far way together - God, Charles and I.

Charles, "thank you for giving to the Lord." I'm so glad God gave me the gift of your love, your prayers and your wise advice through the Lord. I'm glad I'm your son in the ministry! I claim that title and thank God for it! I love you and Debi dearly!

God Bless you always,
Terry Nied

R.K. Rawson

To My Barnabas - Brother of Encouragement

Rev. Charles Ray Grasty has so many gifts from God. He has preached God's Word faithfully at FBC, Neches for twenty years now and continuing. Along the way, God has also given him gifts to pastor the flock, evangelize the lost, comfort the down trodden, challenge the satisfied, and encourage just about all of us, wherever he has found us along life's journey.

I would like to share some memories where my brother Charles has been a living presence as my Barnabas.

I recall how Barnabas was the one God used to formally introduce the newly converted Saul of Tarsus to the other Apostles in Jerusalem. God put within Barnabas the gift of encouragement to allow him to see the potential God was developing within Saul.

Do you remember the days when Promise Keepers got hold of Brother Charles and the others at FBC Neches? The original ten went up to Boulder in the church van, hoping to get a glimpse of God. They all met with God and came back glowing for an entire year as He caused them to continue "glowing" before the rest of us. The transfiguration of those men continued as they prayed together faithfully and gave testimony in many churches. Brother Charles and those who knew these real Promise Keepers also began to pray for other men, like me, by name - asking God to share His glory in their lives also.

A year after the 1993 PK meeting, the fervent prayers of the righteous men of FBC, Neches availed much – 90 other men from our area caught the vision to go and see if God would again show up in Boulder, for them as He had for the original ten. God allowed me to be one of those 90 men. God opened up a seat on the bus just 10 days before departure. It was on the "way up" to Boulder that someone shared that Brother Charles and the others had been praying for me for a year specifically to go to Boulder with them. WOW! If they only know all that God had to overcome to make that happen. I praise God for their prayer vigil that would lead to God's new "calling" on Carla's and me life!

It was on Friday night (July 29, 1994) in Boulder stadium, about 9PM when Jesus came "out of eternity" and visited with me personally. Jesus asked me to surrender all to Him and join Him in ministry. It really was that night that the Lord also began a deep brotherly relationship between Bro. Charles and Me.

It was not until Feb 5th, 1995, that I finally made my answer to Jesus a public "yes" with Carla in full support. In the meantime, Brother Charles had encouraged me to wait for God to do the work in both Carla's and my hearts. Bro. Charles gave me my first preaching opportunity in a Baptist Church. I do not recall the message, but whatever it was, I was surprised God did not kill me! The people of FBC, Neches were so gracious and encouraging - just like their pastor. Since that time I have had the privilege of filling the pulpit at this wonderful church many times.

One thing about Bro. Charles that really blesses me is his perpetual calendar. He keeps annual calendars of spiritual events right there in his office. His calendar wall give record of physical and spiritual birthdates, baptisms, weddings, and departure and funeral dates. What an encouragement this is to children growing up, parents who love for their pastor to remember their kids special dates. If you are ever in doubt of your special date and you are a part of Bro. Charles life, just ask him - he'll know.

He also keeps personal testimonies for his own encouragement and then later he will refer to the person's testimony if someone comes to him with questions about his eternal destiny.

I praise God for Bro. Charles, who has always encouraged me to read the Bible and do what it says. It is a joy to know that there is someone in this life who knows the struggles we are facing on the inside and remains faithful in prayer and action while God brings the answers we need in His timing. By his example, I am able to be this kind of brother to others in the ministry.

On August 6th 1995, I preached both the morning and evening messages at FBC, Neches. Bro. Charles wasn't there, he was in Africa with the Jimmy Hodges Ministries. The first week they were teaching African National Pastors and the second week doing open air evangelistic meetings. God used Bro. Charles to do a deep work in Africa. The trip changed him. I could see it in him and others who went to Africa with him. While Bro. Charles was having that opportunity to preach the Gospel in Africa, God and Bro. Charles encouraged my preaching beginning by allowing me to preach for him. Very interesting that later on God would call me into the very ministry Bro. Charles went off to work with. I now know that God was busily connecting the dots of my calling through the many encouragements of Bro. Charles.

The Country Pastor

In 2003 we both went on mission together to Lusaka, Zambia. Together we prayed, taught, and saw God win thousands of souls into His kingdom.

Bro. Charles started that trip on crutches because of a foot injury. I wondered how he was managing with all the pain he was in. On a later trip I had to travel back from Africa on crutches because of an injury. I remember the pain! This gave me an even deeper appreciation for Bro. Charles fervor to "GO TO" Africa - even if it meant going on crutches to be used of God in the winning of souls.

Bro. Charles you truly are the example that Paul talks about I Romans 12. You are our Brother of Encouragement. Thank you!

K.R. Rawson, Int. Missions Director
Reaching Souls International

A Last Word

As we pay tribute to the man of God, Charles Grasty, we are really paying tribute to Almighty God, who paid a very dear ransom for him. And, No book about Charles Grasty would be complete without giving the reader the opportunity to know -

The Way of Salvation.

1. *All of us have sinned and come short of the Glory of God.* Romans 3:23
2. *The wages of sin is death, but the gift of God is eternal life through His Son, Jesus Christ.* Romans 6:34
3. *If you will confess with your mouth that you Believe in Jesus Christ, and believe in your heart that God raised Him from the dead, you will be saved. For with the heart man believes, resulting in righteousness and with the mouth he confesses, resulting in Salvation.* Romans 10:9-10
4. *As many as received Him, Jesus Christ, to them He gave the right to become children of God.* John 1:12

The Country Pastor

Right Now

We Invite you to say this simple prayer:

"Dear God,

I've known in my head that Jesus is your Son, Now I believe it in my heart. Please forgive me for living my life own way - apart from you. Jesus is the reason I can be right with you. Jesus, thank you for dying for my sins. Come into my life and make me a new person. I thank you that you hear my prayer. I believe your Holy Word - that You now live in my heart. I also ask you to fill me with your Holy Spirit - that I may have all the gifts, power and fruit that will help me be successful in my new life."
In the name of my new Savior, Jesus Christ, I pray.
AMEN

About Mary F. Froese

Mary Francess Froese is an award winning author of three previously published books:

Heroes of a Special Kind, written to honor the more than five hundred thousand volunteer coaches of Special Olympics around the world. She gathered the inspiring stories of these coaches from throughout the United States and Australia.

From Pain to Promise, the Story of Mary Magdalene is a Biblical novel on the early life of the most beloved female disciple of Jesus.

Working in God's Harvest, the Story of Ken Steiner
A California fruit farmer who was given a supernatural gift of healing. He is a soul winner whom God has given incredible opportunities to work in His Harvest.

Retired from San Diego County government, Mary and Allen, her husband of 49 years, live with their beloved son Joel in Vista, California.

The Country Pastor

Mary feels her gift of writing is to be used to tell of the adventures of ordinary people indwelled by an Extraordinary God.

If you know of such a person, or would like additional copies of this book, you may contact her at:

Sistertosister@pacbell.net or at:

(760)726-3614